EVANGELICAL WITNESS

IN SOUTH AFRICA

A Critique of Evangelical Theology and Practice
by South African Evangelicals

EVANGELICAL WITNESS
IN SOUTH AFRICA

A Critique of
Evangelical Theology and Practice
by South African Evangelicals

"Concerned Evangelicals"
Soweto

William B. Eerdmans Publishing Company
Grand Rapids, Michigan

First published 1986 by the Evangelical Alliance (U.K.), London, and
Regnum Books, Oxford, on behalf of "Concerned Evangelicals,"
P.O. Box 200, Dobsonville 1865, Republic of South Africa

This edition published through special arrangement with Regnum Books by
Wm. B. Eerdmans Publishing Co., 255 Jefferson Ave. SE, Grand Rapids,
Mich. 49503

Library of Congress Cataloging-in-Publication Data

Evangelical witness in South Africa.

   1. Evangelicalism — South Africa. 2. Apartheid —
South Africa. 3. Theology, Doctrinal — South Africa.
4. South Africa — Church history. I. "Concerned
Evangelicals" (Johannesburg, South Africa)
BR1642.S6E93   1987   276.8'082   87-17166

ISBN 0-8028-0291-5

Contents

Foreword to
the North American Edition

The expression of the Christian faith is often at its best under adverse circumstances. During times of adversity, the faithful are forced to confess what they really believe. It is instructive to contrast the message of "concerned evangelicals" in South Africa with their counterparts in the United States. The message out of South Africa takes us much closer to the confessions of early Christians as they faced persecution and death.

This document developed out of reflections on the state of emergency (July 1985 to March 1986) in South Africa. The immediate demand for a Christian response came from two events. One was the storming of a school and the arrest of children. The other was the counterviolence of the children at a later date. The document produced by "concerned evangelicals" was not a response to the Kairos document, which had been released in September 1985, even though it was inspired by the same "moment of truth" and the resulting "crisis of faith." The message of the evangelicals grew out of their own discussions and workshops. The unique character of this statement is its attitude of self-criticism as well as its tone of confession and repentance. In my estimation, its mood and direction is the secret of its power.

The South African evangelicals who wrote this document had embarked on a course of earnest internal criticism. They asked: Are we supporting the status quo? Are we in any sense the conscience of the state? To what extent are we unduly influenced by American and European missionaries with a different reality? The purpose of the document is to generate constructive discussions among themselves and to make them more effective in their witness to the gospel in South Africa. Significantly, the term "evangelical" in this context is a comprehensive label including Christians who belong to charismatic and Pentecostal churches as well as charismatic groups within non-Pentecostal churches. This representation includes Christians as diverse as Roman Catholics and members of the African independent churches. In South Africa this is a considerable constituency.

The crisis in South Africa is above all sociopolitical. The state is at war against the poor and oppressed, who are primarily nonwhite. Evangelicals find themselves on the side of the status quo in support of apartheid, a policy of separation. The system is a separate but unequal arrangement with blacks as victims and whites as beneficiaries. This is a state of affairs well-known to blacks in the United States. But there are differences. In South Africa, apartheid is the official policy of the state—while blacks comprise the majority of the population. South Africa exists in a state of government-sponsored repression.

Black Christians in South Africa face a crisis of faith. They are being exploited by white Christians. The atrocities that are committed against them are committed by those who are born again in the name of law and order. The threat of communism is also used to justify the state's repression of blacks. The Bible, especially Romans 13, is being interpreted to support the state's project. Christians, says the state, are to seek heavenly things and accept the powers that be as ordained of God.

Against this background the "concerned Evangelicals" address several concerns in their *Evangelical Witness*.
•   First, say the authors, evangelicals tend to be conservative in their theology. Theology among evangelicals tends to be pride-ridden and legalistic. It does not adequately instruct the faithful for Christian living. It favors the rich and powerful rather than the poor and powerless.

This theology is dualistic in that it sets the earthly and the heavenly over against each other. It dichotomizes the physical and the spiritual. It accepts piety on the spiritual plane as not inconsistent with oppression on the physical plane. Furthermore, Christians who are victimized are to endure dehumanization rather than resist it.

These evangelicals now see these points as distortions of the Christian faith. The gospel of Jesus Christ is subversive—following Jesus demands radical obedience. Dualism is a Greek rather than a biblical concept; biblical faith directs us to live a righteous life in this world while witnessing to the coming kingdom. Both the Jews of the Bible and Africans see religion as embracing all of life.

Under the heading of theological conservatism, the authors examine the concept of reconciliation. This point is especially interesting to me, since I first introduced reconciliation into black theology in the United States. I have now spent many years attempting to "clean up" the meaning of this cardinal Christian affirmation. Reconciliation can be readily misunderstood or used for a devious purpose—especially to gloss over situations of gross injustice with the appearance of sweetness and light.

In South Africa, the Dutch Reformed Church has often been described as the government at prayer. All manner of evil is meted out to the oppressed, all as part of a "holy" crusade. Evangelicals are frequently accomplices to that oppression, because they are unaware of the complexity of social and political conflict. Their fear of communism together with their love for peace leads them to avoid or even condemn any knowledge of or skills in social analysis.

Where there is so much oppression and dehumanization, peace has to be far more than the absence of conflict. In the face of the sin of racism, confession and repentance are prerequisites for forgiveness and reconciliation. In South Africa, there are sins on the side of both the oppressors and the oppressed. The sins of oppression are obvious. But when the oppressed accept the marring of the image of God by the apartheid regime, this, too, is sin. Reconciliation requires sacrifice and pain. In the language of Dietrich Bonhoeffer, reconciliation is a "costly grace." Peace is indeed more than the absence of conflict. There is no real peace without justice. Anytime justice is sought in a situation of injustice, Christians must be prepared to bear the cross.

• Second, evangelicals usually advocate a theology of the status quo. This document makes reference to Luther's "two kingdoms ethic" as well as to the fundamentalist interpretation of Romans 13 I have already mentioned in passing. The Lutheran position has been the subject of endless debate and is too complex to treat here. We might observe, however, that in South Africa the Reformed view of church and state is more troublesome than the Lutheran ethic. Once a state decides on an unjust policy, it will seek to support that policy through whatever theology or ideology is near at hand.

The Romans 13 passage deserves further attention. Are the powers that be always ordained by God? When one has a worthy understanding of God, one sees that, at times, some governments oppose God completely. A problem of exegesis is also crucial here. A *text* must be placed in *context* before it is applied to a contemporary situation. Otherwise the gospel may be preached at the expense of the gospel. In my judgment it is always a sobering matter to compare Revelation 13 to Romans 13. We are reminded as well of some Western missionary responsibility for this truncated understanding of Romans 13. We must acknowledge a great need for a serious examination of how we use the Bible when we see it used to support such an evil social order.

The support that evangelical theology has given to the "law and order" cry of the apartheid system together with the heretical theology in support of the *South African* preamble to the South African constitution illustrate a status quo theology. Confession and repentance are, indeed, called for. It is on this point that the present statement and the Kairos document are mutually reinforcing. There is here a powerful message from South Africa to all Christians.

• The third concern of the concerned evangelicals addresses "structural conformity." This critique follows from the conservative and status quo nature of evangelical theology.

Christians tend to reflect the characteristics of their environment. In fact, Christianity is well-known for its "cultural captivity" to colonialism and racism. South Africa is unique in the extreme nature of its apartheid policy in a postcolonial world. We are here reminded of the powerful influence of "socialization" in South Africa upon the outlook of Christians, black and white.

This is reinforced by the impact of Western culture upon the soul-winning outreach of missionaries in Third World countries. There is a tendency to separate the preaching of the gospel from the pain and suffering that people endure. Missionaries see their role as bringing truth and civilization with the gospel to a "dark" continent. There is a built-in neocolonialism or imperialism that affects missions as well as the geopolitical realities of Third World countries.

Evangelicals are especially vulnerable to the incidence of structural conformity because of their conservative, status quo tendencies. They are apt to remain loyal to denominations and parent churches, usually white. In the South African setting, evangelical black congregations are likely to accept, without question, the evils of that society. In a word, they are conformist institutions. What is called for is a transformation of the society and a renewal of the church.

• Fourth, the authors express their concern for the enormity of the problem of conservatism among the churches in South Africa. This is the result of the sheer abundance of evangelical Christians, in all denominations. The religious situation is such that the phenomena thus far described are widespread and extremely powerful. If the social conditions of injustice and dehumanization are to be changed, there must be a radical reformulation of evangelical faith, thought, and action.

• The fifth concern is the lack of ecumenical outreach. Churches which are theologically, politically, and structurally conservative are not likely to seek interdenominational fellowship and cooperation. Thus there is a great divide between evangelicals and ecumenicals in South Africa. Evangelicals protest the humanistic and "social gospel" aspects of the ecumenical movement. Evangelicals rightly point to a sin as a radical personal reality to be redeemed. They are correct to remind others that salvation cannot be reduced to social involvement. But they need themselves to be reminded that God is at work to save the whole of creation. The gospel is in fact multidimensional. In this instance, social change and individual salvation are two aspects of a holistic salvation.

The internal conflicts among evangelicals are equally devastating. Their sectarianism is inherently parochial. They find it difficult to fellowship and cooperate within their own circles. The openness of the ecumenical movement leads directly to interdenominational and inter-institutional activity, while on the evangelical side, the effort to "fence" the gospel leads to exclusion and discord. Evangelicals saddled with dogmatism, purism, and individualism can scarcely realize genuine community. These factors make it difficult for evangelicals to witness effectively in a hostile society.

• The sixth concern in this document addresses the area of missiology. Evangelicalism takes the great commission seriously—it is zealous that the gospel be preached globally. All Christians should affirm this. But, unfortunately, negative factors often distort this noble purpose. The preaching of the gospel often leads to oppression rather than liberation.

Here the "concerned evangelicals" who signed the statement jolt us once again by their scathing criticism of Western missionaries and evangelists. Exclusively white, these Western preachers are too quick to endorse the stance of the apartheid white regime in South Africa. They preach submissiveness to the social evils there. They go so far as to call it sinful to complain about injustice or to seek equality. It is, in my view, a great disservice to the Christian cause that Western Christian leaders should so distort the gospel in foreign parts. It is a further concern that they should enter the discussion of communism or terrorism in a way to further confuse the issue—which is the official and systematic oppression of nonwhites in South Africa. They also juxtapose capitalism to communism, and, of course, go on to embrace capitalism as being compatible with Christianity. The gospel is thereby allied to the Western political economy.

We have reason to be gravely concerned that Christian leaders from the United States are so deeply involved in this travesty of the gospel. The statement cites, for example, Jimmy Swaggart, who actually sided with the South African government against the interest of suffering blacks in the name of the gospel. South African TV used Swaggart's sermon in an effort to justify the government's repressive measures when it declared the state of emergency on June 12, 1986. In his sermon, Swaggart declared that "apartheid is dead." This arrogant statement angered blacks who experience daily the fact that apartheid is alive and well and that it kills their children. We are reminded also of Jerry Falwell's infamous remark that "Bishop Tutu is a phoney." Here the "concerned evangelicals" have grasped a truth that Mammon rather than God is the motive behind much evangelical missionary activity in the United States and abroad. With the scandal of Jim Bakker in mind, we scarcely need outsiders to remind us.

Black Americans recognize another very familiar point. The "concerned evangelicals" observe that the evangelical missions are foreign and white. The whites who are called to preach to South African blacks are frequently from the United States, where racism is also alive and well. This naturally makes them suspect. They are materialistic and racist at the same time. Thus they are at home in a situation where decision-making authority remains with whites. They not only support apartheid in the state, they also willingly practice it in their religious assemblies.

The "concerned evangelicals" note that the two flags that fly over the

Rhema Centre in Randburg, Johannesburg—the flags of South Africa and the United States—symbolize the support of apartheid by both governments. From the viewpoint of the blacks of South Africa, America is "foreign enemy No. 1."

As an Afro-American, I read this judgment against the United States with some pain. I thought of the commitment of Leon Sullivan, Walter Fauntroy, Randall Robinson, and a host of Americans, white as well as black, who continue to work and sacrifice for justice in South Africa. The fact that blacks in South Africa could generally speak of Americans as "enemies" indicates that there is a lack of communication and that much still needs to be done on their behalf. But this will require openness on the part of blacks in South Africa as well as more effort on our part.

• The seventh and last point of this document treats the radical demands of the gospel. The realities of South Africa demand uncompromising righteousness. The call to repentance is required before there can be a reconciliation with God and other people. But the call to repentance demands social change toward the realization of justice. Evangelicals tend to condemn personal sins—adultery or stealing—while they are too often silent regarding social sin—oppression and exploitation. "Born again" Christians in our country show this distinction in their different levels of concern about lust and greed. Lust is generally associated with personal sin and is regarded as much more serious than greed, which is a merely social sin. But the two are often closely linked; the scandals surrounding American TV evangelists illustrate this fact. When greed is rampant, lust is often near at hand. In South Africa, the radical gospel is directly opposed to apartheid. No partial understanding of the gospel is adequate. Repentance is urgently called for, since the Evangelicals have betrayed this radical faith.

The document concludes with a challenge for a prophetic ministry that could lead to personal and group suffering. The signers advocate casting aside fear and promise themselves to witness boldly to salvation, justice, and peace. They remind us of the kind of faith that gave birth to the Christian faith. The first Christians endured persecution, even death, for the sake of the gospel. The closing words of these evangelicals are forceful and sobering for all Christians: "We have to take a stand now even if it may mean persecution by earthly systems. For if we fail now we shall have no legitimacy in the post-liberation period unless we want to join the hypocrites of this world."

The focus of this document is self-criticism. But this internal reflection is not in the nature of self-flagellation. It is rather aimed at self-correction. The mood is one of confession and repentance, which come before forgiveness, redemptive change, or renewal. The authors have addressed forthrightly one of the greatest handicaps of evangelicals: their own self-righteousness.

The weaknesses and pitfalls they have so carefully examined, as they face what is for them at once a moment of truth and a crisis of faith, deserve careful reading by all Christians. None of us escape many of the concerns they have mentioned, especially in times of testing. It is important that all Christians measure their confession and seek forgiveness from the Lord of the church by the same rigorous standards these evangelicals have discussed.

If there is any flaw in the statement, it is that it is only partially complete. The authors are not able to say exactly what steps they will take to overcome the failings that seem to be endemic to evangelicalism. In a crisis that is indeed sociopolitical as well as religious, a proper understanding of the Bible and theology may not be enough. Evangelicals are usually reluctant to stray far from their theological disciplines. They mention social analysis, but they do not indicate how they will use it, nor do they demonstrate any competence in that direction. I affirm most of what they have accomplished. This is an enlightening, moving, and challenging statement. But I am left wondering where they will go from here. Will evangelicals in South Africa become the conscience of that oppressive state? Will they become in that situation effective voices and means toward the liberation of the oppressed?

J. Deotis Roberts
Professor of Philosophical Theology
Eastern Baptist Theological Seminary
Philadelphia

May 1987

Foreword to
the British Edition

It is easy to criticize others. Finding fault with ourselves is something we find a little more difficult.

Many people accuse evangelicals of a reluctance to be honest about their weaknesses and failings. And some say that evangelicals tend to ignore the social dimensions of the Christian gospel. Whatever truth there may or may not be in these accusations, it is quite certain that they cannot be levelled at this volume.

In one sense, this is a compilation from different viewpoints. In another it is a meeting of minds where brothers and sisters affirm that they are of one spirit together. As such it is symptomatic of a deep move of God among evangelicals.

The nineteenth century evangelical commitment to social activism resulted in orphanages, hospitals, prison visitation, the abolition of slavery and the revision of working hours and conditions for women and children. The old conviction that evangelicals had to be involved in the real world as instruments of change under the hand of God is being reborn. This short book is a testimony to that fact.

It would be simple to whitewash evangelical apathy in the twentieth century. Victories have been won and many people have been brought to a commitment to Jesus. Yet major areas of evangelical conviction have been ignored and salt has sometimes appeared tasteless to society.

For this failure, repentance is necessary in order that new beginnings can be made. We can never be satisfied with merely verbalising the truth of a personal relationship with Jesus Christ—the life that Jesus brings must be lived in the middle of the world in which he has placed us.

Our brothers and sisters in South Africa do not face the same problems which we do. We, in turn, are not in their position either. So we may not wish to agree with every thought and sentiment in this book. Nor do we have to.

We can learn, however, the way to repent of failure, return to our evangelical roots and begin again to make an impact on our society.

Racial abuse, intolerance and prejudice are not dead in Britain. But Jesus died to bring down the wall of partition between God and man and to restore right relationships between us all.

Not only is there no bond or free, Jew or Greek in Christ—there is also no black or white. Reconciliation is the name of our conviction together for evangelicals in this country. May we learn together not just to oppose apartheid elsewhere, but to live out the principles of reconciliation in our own land.

Let us also pray for South Africa, and for those whose courage has brought this message from evangelicals in one land to evangelicals in another.

Clive Calver
General Secretary, Evangelical Alliance
London

Philip Mohabir
Chairman, West Indian Evangelical Alliance
London

December 1986.

Preface

Somewhere around September 1985 a group of 'concerned evangelicals' met to discuss the crisis in South Africa and how it affected their lives, their faith and in particular the evangelistic mission which was usually their pre-occupation. It was during the last state of emergency which lasted for about eight months (July 1985-March 1986). Many people were in detention and people were dying at an alarming rate per day in the country. Curfews were applied in some areas and the security forces were storming into schools and arresting even eight-year-olds.

Whilst this group of concerned evangelicals was meeting in one of the churches in Orlando, Soweto, the security forces stormed into the school next to the church and kids were seen breaking window-panes and escaping through the windows. After that the security forces attacked the second school some two hundred metres from where the church was. Some children were arrested there. The group felt helpless and could not do much about the brutal acts of the security forces. They were heavily armed and entitled to do whatever without question from anybody let alone the courts on the basis of the emergency regulations.

Then came the second scene when the school kids became angry about what the security forces did, took to the streets and identified whatever 'manageable' targets they could find, given that they were not armed. They stoned a commercial vehicle, stopped it, let the driver go and attempted to put it on fire. As this second scene occurred we agonized about our role in this situation. If we failed to intervene in the legalized brutal violence of the security forces what right do we have to intervene in the counter-violence of the kids? On the other hand the African National Congress (ANC) had called for a people's war in 1986 to defend people against the security forces of apartheid South Africa which they said were killing defenceless people in the townships. What was our response supposed to be in this situation as evangelical Christians in South Africa?

Moreover the situation was no more conducive to mass evangelistic campaigns and revivals. We could not execute our mission or fulfil our calling to the ministry as we were expected to do. In the meantime there

17

was the draft of the Kairos Document[1] in circulation for discussion about the very situation in the country, albeit from a different theological perspective. After discussing the draft we felt that instead of responding to the Kairos Document from an evangelical theological perspective we should rather address ourselves to the Kairos (moment of truth, crisis) evangelical Christians were going through in the country as outlined above.

Our frustration was that our own churches, groups or organizations were almost lost and could not provide prophetic light in the situation. At the worst most would be supporting the status quo instead of being a conscience to the state. We felt that although our perception of the gospel helped us to be what we are, saved by the blood of the Lord Jesus Christ, born again into the new family of the Kingdom of God, our theology nevertheless was inadequate to address the crisis we were facing. In our series of discussions subsequent to this meeting we realized that our theology was influenced by American and European missionaries with political, social and class interests which were contrary or even hostile to both the spiritual and social needs of our people in this country.

Having realized that there was something wrong with the practice and theology of evangelicals in this country we felt God's calling to us to rectify this situation for the sake of the gospel of the Lord. We felt that we as evangelicals had a responsibility of cleaning our house before we try to clean other people's houses. The text of Matt. 7:3–5 impressed itself heavily on us even in terms of trying to critique the Kairos Document. We felt we could not even attempt to remove the speck in our brothers' and sisters' eyes, before we dealt with the log in our own eyes. We have undertaken therefore to critique our own theology and practice, not to disparage our faith, but to turn it into an effective evangelical witness in South Africa today.

This critique has developed over a period of about nine months from September 1985 to June 1986. This involved a series of meetings, discussion groups, workshops and seminars, firstly around Soweto and then extended to the Pretoria–Witwatersrand–Vaal (PWV) area. A draft of all the concerns of these groups of evangelicals was compiled in April 1986 and circulated to as many known evangelicals as possible who are known at least to have the same concerns around the country. The final form was then discussed in June 1986, to be made available for publication.

We therefore humbly present this document to all evangelicals here and abroad to use it as a basis of re-examining our ways to see whether we are still doing the will of our Father or are consciously or

---

1. The *Kairos Document*—a theological comment on the political crisis in South Africa—was produced by 150 theologians meeting in Soweto in 1985. It is available from Wm. B. Eerdmans (U.S.A.), and BCC or The Paternoster Press (U.K.).

unconsciously busy with somebody's agenda rather than the agenda of the Lord. We hope that this document will generate constructive discussions amongst evangelical Christians to sharpen their theological tools to enable them to be effective in their ministry and to respond accordingly to the crisis we are facing in this country.

We also subject this document to the broader ecumenical family, which we cannot ignore, for them to also respond accordingly to our agony which we believe they are also going through.

Lastly, we want to clarify our usage of the word 'evangelical' to avoid misunderstanding and confusion as to who is referred to here. We are using this term in a broad sense including those Christians who belong to the charismatic and pentecostal churches and groups.

'Concerned Evangelicals'
JOHANNESBURG
July 1986

1. Crisis

All of us have been severely taxed by the socio-political crisis of our time. Indeed, some more than others, as the death and injury toll in the Township[1] has continued to escalate in spite of our hopes to the contrary, while state repression and harassment has continued unabated.

Called as we are to minister good news, we find ourselves in the midst of bloodshed and death, of increasing bitterness and polarization, and of rising anger in the townships. Our proclamation therefore, has been swallowed up by the cries of the poor and oppressed that it is now even impossible to hold conventional evangelistic campaigns in this war situation. These voices have become so loud that it has become impossible to hear the church preach.

It is in the light of these facts, that we, a group of Evangelicals, clergy and laity, have come together, praying and agonizing together over the issues of our times. We have (in our discussions and meetings since September 1985) critically reviewed our role as evangelical Christians in South Africa and elsewhere. We wish to confess that to a large extent the evangelical community has chosen to avoid that burden of the socio-political crisis in the country. Or at worst, this community we are so committed to, has chosen to take sides in support of the apartheid system in South Africa which is responsible for the violence that is engulfing our country.

We wish to confess that our evangelical family has a track record of supporting and legitimating oppressive regimes here and elsewhere. That this family has tended to assume conservative positions which tend to maintain the status quo.

We wish to confess that the people who regard themselves as evangelicals across all the churches in South Africa condemn and campaign against all efforts to change the racist apartheid system in South Africa. They condemn and campaign against organizations (ecclesiastical and secular) which engage either in relief (aid) ministries to victims of apartheid or direct programmes to remove the apartheid regime.

Besides the crisis in the country, Black Christians (especially those

---

1. Soweto

who are evangelicals) in the townships are facing a *crisis of faith*. This crisis of faith is caused by the contradictions they have to live with on a daily basis as they try to live their faith in this crisis situation. This crisis of faith is caused by the dilemma of being oppressed and exploited by people who claim to be Christians, especially those who claim to be 'born-again'. It is a dilemma of being detained by these people, tortured and even killed by them in the name of 'Law and Order' or in the name of combating 'communism'.

This crisis is worsened by the support of the apartheid regime by most evangelical churches and groups which oppose any resistance against the apartheid regime reverting all the time to Romans 13, the concepts of reconciliation, love, humility, peace, non-violence and heavenly concerns rather than earthly concerns. The dilemma of the young people we have to minister to in the townships is further worsened by the fact that the whole Christian family, the so-called Christian West, support these positions. For this reason it is not possible in the townships to look at 'communism' critically because those who speak against communism are almost all the time those who are responsible for their misery, pain, suffering and death.

We could not help it but to be suspicious of the intentions and interests of members of this our family in their zeal to save the world. To remain faithful to the Lord, we are compelled to critique this position to eliminate the contradictions created for those we are called to minister to, and, to expose the interests of those who maintain this position whose interests seem to be above or beside those of the gospel.

In critiquing our theology (evangelical theology) we have identified seven broad areas of concern:

(1)   The area of basic theological problems like evangelical conservatism, dogmatism, dualism, reconciliation, justice and peace,

(2)   The theology of the status quo: that is, the theology which is used to support and maintain existing systems in the world,

(3)   Oppressive structures of evangelical churches and organizations and their tendency to conform or take the form of the world around them, even when this compromises the very gospel of the Lord,

(4)   Conservative church groups across all the churches in South Africa which claim to be evangelicals,

(5)   The lack of ecumenism, that is, interfellowship and co-operation even among evangelicals,

(6)   The interests, motives and the theology of mission and evangelism of evangelistic groups both locally and internationally as a characteristic of evangelicalism,

(7)   The radical demands of the gospel as opposed to the conservative tendencies of evangelical groups.

These areas have been singled out as the most pertinent of the problems of evangelicals. In our analysis of these areas we intend to trigger an ongoing action and reflection process which will help us to sharpen our theological tools to be able to live our faith in the difficult situation in which we find ourselves. Our main aim is to be alive to God's will for us and what he is calling us to.

We are conscious of what Jesus said to his disciples when he sent them to the world that we are sent out as 'sheep in the midst of wolves', and, for this reason we need to be as 'wise as serpents' (Matt. 10:6). We want to attain maturity of faith, 'to the measure of the stature of the fulness of Christ, *so that we may no longer be children, tossed to and fro and carried about with every wind of doctrine,* by the cunning of men, by their craftiness in deceitful wiles' (Eph. 4:13–14). We want to speak the truth in love, 'to grow up in every way into him who is the head, into Christ' (verse 15).

We are also aware that because of our witness we may be delivered up to councils and flogged in the 'synagogues of Satan'. We are aware that we may be dragged before governors and kings for the sake of the Lord, and, there we shall bear testimony of our faith and the Spirit of the Father shall speak through us (Matt. 10:17–18). When this happens we shall not be surprised or fall away because our Lord has warned us that '. . . the hour is coming when whoever kills you will think he is offering service to God. And they will do this because they have not known the Father nor me' (John 16:1–4).

2. An Overview of Theological Problems in Evangelicalism

Evangelicals in South Africa, as elsewhere, have been at the crossroads for too long reacting to situations rather than leading to the course of events in the world to work towards the Kingdom of God. They have removed themselves from the world, which they call sinful and not worthy of anything except hellfire. Because of this view of life and the world they cannot see any purpose in attempting to change it but rather they are more concerned about saving as many souls as possible from this world. Otherwise they are just waiting for the Lord to come and take them to his abode, to rest, in heaven.

· Although they are aware that 'God so loved the world that he gave his only son' (John 3:16) for it, to give it life, and life more abundantly (John 10:10) they have abandoned the world because it is too sinful for them. Their living for Christ in this world is an interim measure that prepares them for heaven. Real life here is meaningless, trying to bring about changes in this world is occupying oneself with earthly things. This view of evangelicals differs radically from the approach of Christ and most of the Jewish traditions during the time of Christ (Sadducees, Pharisees and the Zealots). It is actually closer to the Essenes who withdrew from public life to keep true to their ancestors' faith. They had an ascetic tendency, calling all others 'children of darkness'.

Evangelicalism and Conservatism

Somehow, because of this attitude about the world and this cock-eyed theological perception, evangelicals tend to be conservative. They are pre-occupied with the struggle of conserving the remaining 'truths' about the gospel by living an exemplary life within which there is nothing wrong. But there is always a tendency to want a few explicit rules to follow in their spiritual sojourn. In the quest for these rules evangelicals have gone off the extreme, at the conservative end. There is in the first instance the tendency to legalism which leads to pride, and an inadequate theology about Christian living. Legalism provides support for a conservative and exclusive lifestyle, which is in contrast to the lifestyle of Jesus. In fact, evangelicals go to great lengths claiming Jesus did not teach what he clearly did. We have to, because to admit he taught what he did, would require us either to change (repent) or to criticize him. And neither of these are acceptable. So we opt to discolour the lifestyle of Jesus.

But this approach is contrary to the very gospel of salvation, which requires us to be born again, to be renewed, to create new beings in Christ. The problem is that Jesus was radical, always geared to turning the world upside down. He did not turn the world upside down from the top for the benefit of the affluent and the powerful in the Jewish society. This would be superversion. But he turned the world upside down from below for the benefit of the poor and powerless (subversion). He challenged the rich young man to sell what he had and give to the poor to be able to follow him (Matt. 19:16–30); he ate with tax collectors and sinners (Matt. 9:10–13); he broke the Sabbath (12:10–14). For Jesus the first shall be last and the last shall be first (Mark 9:35), whoever is great must be a servant, and whatever is first must be the slave of all (Mark 10:43–45). To Jesus the penny contributed by the poor widow is more than all the large contributions of the rich (Mark 10:41–44). In addition he called Herod a 'fox' (Luke 13:32). We would go on and on to learn about the subversive gospel of the Lord Jesus Christ.

Even his followers, the Christians of Acts 17:6, were described as those who have 'turned the world upside down'. The problem is that Jesus was a radical and we are moderates. He was committed to a radical change and we are committed to moderation, to reformist liberal tendencies which leave the system intact. Jesus talked about losing life to gain life and giving one's life for others like he did for us, whilst we are concerned about our interests and the preservation of our lives. To follow Jesus in word and deed therefore means to be radical and not conservative.

Dualism

The concept of dualism is more of a Greek philosophical concept than a biblical concept. The Greek philosophers believed in a clear demarcation between the spiritual and material. They believed that all material things were evil whilst God was a Spirit somehow committed to save the spirit in the bodies of human beings. On the basis of this Greek philosophical concept of dualism western theologians saw the gospel as concerned only with the spiritual rather than the social. They dichotomized between the physical and the spiritual and between the sacred and secular. Evangelical theologians have bought wholesale into this model of dualism.

The consequences of this dualistic form of life has been disastrous for evangelical faith. What this dualism has done is that one can live a pietistic 'spiritual' life and still continue to oppress, exploit, and dehumanize people. And those who are victims of this oppression, exploitation and dehumanization are prohibited from complaining or resisting it because this would amount to worrying about material things that have nothing to do with one's spirituality. Actually trying to engage in a struggle to get rid of this oppression is seen as having 'fallen' from grace. In this way the oppressors of this world are able to maintain their system by conveniently confining the gospel to the spiritual realm alone. It is just like keeping the gospel in captivity to be able to continue in sin without any disturbance to their consciences. Like the Sadducees and Pharisees, we are claiming the authority of the written law but we refuse to let it address the real issues of our day.

This concept of dualism is also applied in trying to differentiate between 'heavenly' things and 'earthly' things. Here for instance, blacks are told to worry only about heavenly things whilst others, claiming to be Christians, dispossess them of their land and enslave them to make profits out of them. This is a hypocritical type of gospel. We believe that whereas all Christians must look forward to a future Kingdom where Jesus will reign, where peace, justice and righteousness will prevail— call it heaven—the fact of the matter is that we are still in this world and we have to eat, be clothed, be housed, etc. We still need to have our children go to school and be taken care of. When Jesus was about to ascend to his Father he did not pray that his disciples follow him immediately, he did not pray that God take them out of the world but he prayed that God should keep them from the evil one (John 17:15). What is important now is to live a righteous life in this world and to be a witness to the coming Kingdom of God.

The Judeo-Christian faith as found in the Bible is different from Greek dualism. It does not differentiate between the spiritual and the social because Jews live their spiritual life in their social life. For the Israelites being oppressed was a concern of their God. When they went to war their God had to be involved or they would be doomed. Their cultural life was a spiritual life. Their economic life was a spiritual life (the Jubilee, the question of loans, etc.). Their political life was a spiritual life (appointment of kings and deposing of kings, how they ruled etc.). There was nothing for the Jews that was not spiritual in their whole lives. There was no reserved room in their lives which was not spiritual which could keep their sins. It was all spiritual.

The African form of spirituality is also the same. For an ordinary African birth, death, employment and unemployment, having a house and not having a house, being sick, attacked or not having money, all had to do with the Supreme Being called Modimo, Unkulunkulu, Tixo, etc. Their ancestors (bodimo, etc.) were understood as being involved in everything that affected them in all aspects of life. The concept of dualism is therefore a foreign concept to both the African and the Judeo-Christian traditions. This is not a biblical concept. It is but a Greek and Western concept.

The Problem of the Concept of Reconciliation

Faced with this trouble-torn country, faced with the war between the apartheid regime and the oppressed masses, faced with the ideological conflicts which are tearing our communities apart, and confronted with the possibility of a revolution, our response and choices will determine the future of our Christian faith in this country.

It is doubtful whether for most evangelicals the real underlying religious issue is clearly visible. On the contrary, the average evangelical seems to react in much the same way as the average agnostic or pagan. The interests of the State and the Church are all confused with one another. In fact, some of our evangelical leaders have actively joined in the cold war and called God to justify the moral blindness and outrageous deeds of generals and industrialists, and to bless shootings and killings as a holy and apocalyptic crusade. To use the cliché of Vietnam days, 'Shoot a commie for Jesus'; in South Africa we hear more and more that 'no price is too high to pay for our religious liberty'.

Even the legislation here not only permits self-defence for those in power but also legislates retaliation which may exceed the amount of the original attack so that the aggressor 'learns a lesson'. This may sound noble, perhaps to those who are not shocked by its all too evident meaninglessness. The fact is that genocide is too high a price, and no one, not even evangelicals, not even for the highest ideals, has the right to take measures that might destroy millions of innocent non-combatants.

That we as Christians have to be peacemakers here is very clear (Matt. 5:9). But how we make this peace is a serious problem especially when we are part of the problem. It is here that the most bedevilling concept, that of reconciliation, arises. The basic text we use here is usually 2 Cor. 5:18–20 which reads:

> . . . God . . . through Christ reconciled us to himself and gave us the ministry of reconciliation, that is, in Christ God was reconciling the world to himself, not counting their trespasses against them, and entrusting to us the message of reconciliation . . . We beseech you on behalf of Christ, be reconciled to God.

Whilst Rom. 5:10 affirms that 'while we were enemies we were reconciled to God by the death of his Son,' some amongst the evangelical family believe that one just needs to preach the gospel more to get more people to be reconciled to God so that they can also be reconciled to other human beings. Well, this is good and in keeping with the gospel but it is not necessarily the solution to our problem. There is no guarantee that all or the majority of South Africans will accept the gospel to effect reconciliation. What is worse is that those we thought were the ones who are 'born again' and 'reconciled' to God have turned out to be the worst racists, oppressors and exploiters. We are committed to preaching the gospel of reconciliation at all costs for the sake of the Kingdom of God, but we are aware that this is just part of the solution and not the whole solution.

Some believe that we must bring together the warring groups to reconcile them. This may sound good but there are serious problems involved here. Firstly, most Christians, especially evangelicals, have very little understanding of conflict or of the skills of conflict resolution. It is worse when it comes to political or social conflicts because they have no understanding of both political and social dynamics. Most of the time they are not directly involved themselves and have no understanding of the situation. They have no social understanding of ideological dynamics in these struggles. They are for instance quick to condemn communism without any reading or understanding about it. No social analysis is done to understand the dynamics involved. This problem is complicated by the arrogance of most Christians, especially evangelicals, who believe they know better than everyone else because of the 'grace of the Lord'. They ignore the experiences of those who are involved in these situations because they believe these people are sinners and therefore lost. They cannot see any good that can come out of them.

The next real problem is how reconciliation is effected. The weakness with our approach is that we use the word reconciliation simply as a slogan and hope that reconciliation will take place. No sloganizing is going to effect it.

We believe that there is only one way in which reconciliation can be effected. The reconciliation between God and us, for instance, takes place only when we accept God's offer of salvation by faith, confessing our sins, so that our trespasses are not counted against us. In John 1:9 we read that:

> If we confess our sins, he is faithful and just, and will forgive our sins and cleanse us from unrighteousness.

It is clear here that reconciliation goes hand in hand with repentance where there is consciousness about one's sins, leading to confession followed by forgiveness and cleansing. This is the only way in which South Africans can be reconciled. Firstly we must all be conscious of the sin that has led us to this war. The sin of racism. The sin of undermining other people as if they were not made in the very image of God. The sin of discriminating against other people and suppressing them to stop them from utilizing their potential and living their lives in full. The sin of dispossessing people of their land. The sin of accumulating riches by making profits at the expense of other vulnerable humans, by so doing impoverishing them. The sin of classism and sexism. The sin of monopoly of power where people want 'reforms' that will leave them still in power; the 'power sharing' that will guarantee white control in South Africa. These are the sins of white South Africa—which sins they need to confess and repent from, so that there can be forgiveness and reconciliation.

The sins that black South Africa must confess are those of complacence and permissiveness in the face of sin that reduced the image of God in them into nothingness. Their failure to listen to God and to follow the demands of the gospel. Their failure to minister to white South Africans to repent from their sin of racism. Their failure to preach the gospel against the evil of tribalism in the form of tribal Bantustans which apartheid South Africa has imposed on them. The sin of failure to exercise their love for white South Africa by liberating them from their fears because of their agelong sin. The sin of simply bottling up with anger and bitterness without opening up to be used by God. The sin of fear of harassment, detention, torture, long imprisonment, assassination and death.

It is clear that reconciliation will not happen without sacrifice and pain. Reconciliation at times goes with tears. Some of us may have to be 'sacrificial' lambs to effect reconciliation. It is clear that reconciliation is not possible without repentance, confession of sins and forgiveness. Any reconciliation which happens without repentance cannot be reconciliation. This is tantamount to reconciling sin with righteousness, evil with good. It is trying to reconcile the devil with God. Is this not a hypocritical form of reconciliation? No compromise with evil is possible in terms of our evangelical faith and thus we must work for real and genuine reconciliation in South Africa. Repentance on the one hand and forgiveness on the other are essential components of reconciliation.

Justice and Peace

From the discussion of the concept of reconciliation, repentance, confession and forgiveness, it should not be difficult to understand that there can be no peace without justice. That justice can occur only if sin is eradicated in our society. People usually talk about peace as if peace can happen without justice. Stopping people from fighting is not the solution to the problem, but facing the questions of justice and injustice is the only way to produce real peace.

It must therefore be our mission to work for justice to be able to produce peace in this our land.

3. Theology of the Status Quo

Most evangelical groupings, with their narrow view of life and their fundamental approach to the Bible, tend to uncritically support existing oppressive systems. Most of them consciously or unconsciously adhere to Luther's notion of the two Kingdoms: the secular order and the spiritual order which never mix. They argue that the church has nothing to say about this secular order or this earthly kingdom.

Evangelicals are also inclined to the so-called doctrine of creation which takes creation as given and uses slogans like 'it is written', 'it is historical', 'it is ordained by God'. This doctrine works for restoration of the old order rather than for renewal. It also talks about prophecy, that is, 'it is prophesied', meaning that it is futile to try to effect or work for change within a situation if it was prophesied. At times struggling for justice is seen as struggling against God or prophecy. In South Africa for instance segregation of races is tied to this ordinance of creation as developed by the Afrikaans Reformed Churches and enforced by law by the Apartheid Regime. Most evangelical churches have uncritically adopted this doctrine of separation which is discussed under 'Evangelicalism and Conformity'. This theology is prone to support and perpetuate the status quo.

Romans 13

Theologians of the status quo, or State Theology, can be characterized by their use and misuse of Rom. 13. Whenever victims of oppression try to raise their voices or resist the oppression Romans 13 is thrown into their faces by beneficiaries of these oppressive systems. Romans 13 is used therefore to maintain the status quo, and make Christians feel guilty when challenging injustices in society.

With their fundamentalist approach to the Bible evangelicals tend to read Romans 13 to mean that one cannot resist or question any government or authority because it comes from God or it is ordained by God. The context or background of this text is completely ignored and, more so, it is not read to the end to understand the whole message Paul was communicating. No reference is made to other related texts in the Bible to help clarify this text.

The problem here is that those who interpret and preach this view of Romans 13 are mostly those who are part of or beneficiaries of the said government or authority, who detest any attempt to rock the boat which could make them sink. And those of us who are the victims or underdogs of society who hold this view, are just victims of circumstances, completely under the influence of the powerful and oppressors of this world, good students of racist missionaries!

Our understanding of Romans 13 is that although governments are 'ordained' by God what these governments *do* is not necessarily from God and at times can be completely opposed to God. And should this happen as it is with racist and apartheid South Africa, we are bound to say with Peter and John that we shall 'obey God rather than man' (Acts 5:29), because it is not right in the sight of God to listen to man rather than to God. 'For we cannot but speak of what we have seen and heard' (Acts 4:19–20).

The whole Old Testament tradition contradicts blind obedience to oppressive and unjust systems. One could start from Pharaoh through the prophets to the times of Christ and then to the early churches as we have shown above. No, Romans 13 does not call for blind obedience to all evil systems. It is racist missionaries, colonialists and theologians of the West and their churches who developed this tradition to maintain Western domination and imperialism. Rom. 13 defines the nature of an ordained government that has to be obeyed. It says that governments are not a terror to the people but punish wrongdoers (Rom. 13:3–4). The South African regime as we are experiencing it is just the opposite of what Paul said.

We have experienced the South African regime as a terror to the black majority in South Africa. It has silenced those who peacefully voiced • their resentment of the brutality of the apartheid system. It has silenced those who championed the course of justice in South Africa and rather turned on the voices of segregation, dehumanization of blacks, and the voices of those who preach inequality between blacks and whites and of deprivation of human rights for blacks in this country. We have experienced the South African regime as a terrorist regime which raided blacks during the night for permits and passes and which detains our people, tortures them, kills them and imprisons them for working for a just order. To us it is a government that legalizes wrongdoing and punishes right doers.

For even a better understanding of Romans 13 and Paul, we also need to recapture or reconstruct, from various other sources, the circumstances during the time of Paul which caused him to write and communicate this text (letter) to the Roman Congregation (Church). That is, we need to understand the *context* of the *text*. This context does not only refer to the understanding of the whole text but it also refers to the historical circumstances of the time which prompted Paul to address this issue.

Scholars who have researched on this historical context say that Paul was addressing himself to those who so believed that Jesus is their only Lord and King that no other person or government could exercise authority over them. They were subject only to their Lord Jesus Christ. They were defying any form of authority, whether good or bad, because they had only one Lord who had the only authority over them. This group of people was called the 'antinomians' (those who maintained that the moral law is not binding on Christians) or 'enthusiasts' (about the new faith they received). They misused the Lordship of Jesus.

Paul was thus saying that even if Jesus is your only Lord you are still subject to other forms of authority like governments because they are not a terror to good works in any way—but only if they are not against good works.

It is still strange to us how evangelicals call for a blind obedience to all governments as a scriptural demand and in the same breath call for the subversion and condemnation of the so-called 'communist' governments. If anyone has the right to raise a finger against 'communist' governments, then others must also have the same right of condemning and subvertin̈ the racist apartheid regime of South Africa.

We believe that Christians are a critique of the world by their lives, practice and mission, and must retain this critical relationship at all times. Born again Christians must always be dissatisfied about the world, and with existing orders or systems. They must challenge the status quo at all times. They must not be static but they must be dynamic in the direction of radical change. We believe that God, through Jesus Christ, is calling us to salvation, to a radical change of our lives and therefore to a radical change of structures of our society. We believe that we are called to effect these changes. To us it is not a matter of what political system or party is involved but it is a question of how just the system is and how compatible it is to the gospel.

Some enthusiastic missionary evangelists argue that they cannot critique whatever order they find because that would jeopardise their ministry. That is, they may be deported (if they are foreigners) or silenced. For the sake of the gospel they say, we must not interfere with those in power. This position to us actually means preaching the gospel at the expense of the gospel. It means leaving sin to prevail in society to be able to preach against sin. What a contradiction! It is for this reason that oppressed people are rejecting the gospel in their struggles for liberation because of the collaboration of most western pioneers of the gospel with oppressive systems in the two thirds world (Third World).

The worst position is that of those evangelicals who even bribe existing systems for favours to preach the gospel. This is done by creating cordial relationships with these oppressive systems, giving presents to them and helping to legitimize them by developing a theology of the status quo, justifying these systems theologically or biblically. For instance in the celebrations of the so-called independence of Bantustans some of these groups participated actively to promote these systems. This is supported by prophetic messages (at times using tongues and interpretation in pentecostal circles) which assure oppressive systems (governments) of God's protection virtually against all those who oppose them however unjust these systems can be. The criteria here is always support or sympathy for the West rather than the truths of the gospel.

'Law and Order'

Evangelical theology with its conservative and legalistic tendencies accepts the call of the apartheid regime for 'Law and Order' uncritically without assessing the type of 'law' and the type of 'order' this evil system is talking about. It does not assess whether this 'law' and this 'order' are in line with the gospel of the Lord Jesus Christ or whether they negate the gospel.

The fact of the matter is that this 'law' is the unjust law of apartheid which treats blacks as subhumans (less than the image of God) and this 'order' is the orderly way in which the apartheid regime wants to enforce these unjust laws of apartheid. This 'law and order' means that the oppressed and exploited masses of South Africa must orderly and peacefully submit to their oppressors and exploiters.

This to us is the law of Satan and the order of hell. This, in the name of Jesus, we must resist! It is just part and parcel of the theology of the status quo.

The Blasphemous Preamble of the South African Apartheid Constitution

The preamble of the Constitution of the racist apartheid regime of South

Africa is typical of a status quo theology position where God is praised
for helping whites (because of superiority of arms) to dispossess the
aboriginors of this country. It is a theology that takes sides with the
powerful in society who oppress the weak, the orphans, the widows and
the poor contrary to biblical demands (Is. 1:16–17). We quote part of
this preamble to give an idea of this heretic theology of the status quo.

> In humble submission to Almighty God, who controls the destinies of peoples
> and nations, who gathered our forebears together from many lands and gave
> them this their own; who has guided them from generation to generation;
> who has wondrously delivered them from the dangers that beset them.

It is presumptuous on the part of this racist government to claim that it
was the God of the Scriptures who 'gathered' Whites from Europe to
South Africa whereas it is common knowledge that they settled here for
economic reasons. This 'God' referred to in this preamble comes across
as the god of the oppressor to black people in South Africa. It is a 'God' of
the white people of South Africa. To the township youths who are
attacked and killed, this 'God' is the god of the teargas, bullets,
sjamboks, prison cells and death. This type of God to us Christians
comes as an antichrist, negating the very basis of our Christian faith. We
are therefore jealous of the misuse of the name of our God on the
constitution of this apartheid system. It is blasphemous against our God
and all God-fearing born-again Christians must campaign for the
exclusion of this reference to our God in this constitution or otherwise
work for a just society in South Africa which will purge it of this
blasphemous preamble.

4. Evangelicalism and Structural Conformity

Whereas there is a general tendency of the church to conform to the
norms and values of the society of its time even when they are at variance
with the gospel of the Lord Jesus Christ, the evangelical tradition excels
in this regard. It is a fact that our faith is expressed in the language or
idiom of the time of the Bible. It is expressed in terms of symbols,
concept and structures of the time. It is expressed in the culture of the
time. And because of this reality our faith tends to be embedded within
the jungle of the time to an extent that the gospel gets lost in this jungle.
This applies to any time, even our times. Because of the inadequacy of
our language, idiom, symbols, concepts, structures and culture to
express the truths and mysteries of the gospel of the Lord Jesus Christ,

we can now see only dimly through a mirror and we know in part but one day, face to face with God, we shall understand fully (1 Cor. 13:12–13).

We must therefore be conscious of how the society around us influences us and even distorts our thinking. We must be conscious of how our upbringing, or socialization, affects our perception of life. A good example is how radically different the perceptions of whites and blacks are of the South African reality. It is for this reason that we could read the same text and hear different messages from it because our eyes, ears and our brains are geared to seeing, hearing and understanding things in terms of our socialization.

Because of the influence of the West, because of the perceptions of western Christians the wave of colonization as a victory for the missionary enterprise and the spread of what they called Christian civilization, most of the missionaries could not see the evils of colonization. They could not see the brutalization of the aborigines of the lands they were colonizing. In fact when the colonialist gained victory against the aborigines of these lands and subdued them the missionaries saw an opening for the christianization of those people.

In the same way evangelicalism, being rooted in the U.S.A. and Europe, is blind to western domination and exploitation of the peoples of the Third World. What they see is more of winning souls for Christ rather than the pain and suffering the people are going through. Because of this insensitivity and lack of awareness on the part of these white missionaries about the oppressive nature of their tradition and culture they have transplanted this oppressive culture into the church.

Today we have these crude missionary attitudes of colonial times still prevalent in evangelical circles. For instance they still see blacks as the 'mission field' and whites as the bearers of truth and civilization. They still see Africa as a 'dark' continent which needs the gospel when there are more 'lapsed' Christians or non-Christians in Europe and in white South Africa.

But conformity of evangelicals in terms of proportion is seen more in the structures of their churches, organizations and movements. They are dominated and controlled by whites with heavy paternalistic tendencies. They are structured according to the apartheid norms of our society. One hears more of concepts like 'mother' churches and 'daughter' churches in evangelical circles. One hears more of concepts like the 'white church' the 'coloured church' the 'Indian church' and the 'African church' within evangelicalism. And those African, Coloured and Indian churches, so-called, are usually under the control of the White church of that particular denomination. Because of these lines of white control, black congregations in the townships are not able to minister to the people there according to their needs. For them to address the conflict situation according to the way God calls them to do, usually means victimization from the dominant white block. As a result evangelicals are paralyzed in the townships, and unable to carry the message of the gospel to the people.

When South Africa is divided according to apartheid norms evangelicals normally move swiftly, without question, to redefine their boundaries to conform with this apartheid development. In fact their structures are a mirror of the evil reality of our society. We are ashamed of the structures of our tradition which are also an indictment to us.

Maybe we need to recall Paul's appeal, two thousand years ago, not to be *conformed* to this world but to be *transformed* by the renewal of our minds, that we may prove what is the good and acceptable and perfect will of God (Rom. 12:2). We pray that evangelicals face the gospel truth that Jesus has broken down the dividing walls of hostility, by abolishing in his flesh the law of commandments and ordinances, that he might create in himself a new humanity in place of the two, so making peace, making us fellow citizens with the saints and members of the household of God, in whom (Jesus) the whole structure is joined together and grows into a holy temple in the Lord (Eph. 2:11–22).

5. Evangelicalism and Conservatism

In South Africa there are evangelical groups in every church from the Roman Catholic Church to African Independent Churches, with the so-called evangelical and pentecostal churches being the chief bearers of this phenomenon. These groups and related churches tend to all assume conservative positions with a blanket support of the South African apartheid regime. They are so obsessed and pre-occupied with what they call the 'threat of communism' to the extent of blessing any regime in the world that is anti-communist, however evil and corrupt it may be. They have put their eyes so much on their conception of the 'evil' of communism that they cannot see the evils of the systems within which they are living, and, in most cases they are part of the perpetrators or beneficiaries of these systems.

It is strange that these individuals, groups and churches can see the speck in their brothers' and sisters' eyes but cannot detect the log in their own eyes. They are fast and swift in attempting to take out this speck without even worrying about the log in their eyes (Matt. 7:3–5). In fact it is strange that they feel 'comfortable' with this log in their eyes. It is this very eye which is blinded by the log, the evils of apartheid, through which they want to see the evils of communists. It is for this reason that Jesus called them 'hypocrites'. Listen to what Jesus says:

> You hypocrites, first take the log out of your eyes, and then you will see clearly to take the speck out of your brother's eye (Matt. 7:5).

In fact they need the power of the blood of the Lord Jesus Christ to enable them to remove this log. Our focus therefore must be to preach the gospel to help South Africans to remove the log in their eyes before we even talk about 'Communism'. (That does not mean that we endorse totalitarian Marxism or overlook the evils it too has perpetuated in the modern world.)

To these groups and churches what is called western Christian civilization or the western capitalistic culture is seen as identical with the Christian faith or the demands of the gospel. Any other system (especially economic) which is not necessarily capitalist is taken as being atheistic and therefore anti-christian. In their understanding of their faith they cannot see a possibility of being socialist and also Christian. Tragically these Christians miss the biblical obligation to measure and critique all systems, capitalist, socialist, marxist etc. on the basis of biblical norms.

The most striking element of these groups/churches, which is an inherent part of their mode of operation, is that they are always silent about the evils of the South African apartheid regime and its necessary violence to maintain it. They are quiet about the oppression and exploitation of millions of South African Blacks and are not moved by the pain, misery and suffering, blacks are subjected to. But if the victims of this system raise their voice to resist this system, the voices of condemnation from these conservative evangelical groups become the loudest. These are the voices we have heard condemning prophetic church leaders like Bishop D. Tutu, Dr. A. Boesak, Dr. B. Naude and Archbishop D. Hurley, amongst many others.

We wish to put on record that even if we may have differences with some of these church leaders we believe that their efforts and convictions are more honest than the evangelical groups which condemn and attack them. We are disgusted by the hypocrisy of these groups, seen in their doing nothing about the pain and suffering of the people and attacking those who are doing whatever within their power as given by God to change this apartheid system to avoid a blood-bath in this country.

We are convinced that the western capitalist culture has become an idol of these groups. It has become their god which they so love and worship. We are also convinced that there are other interests than those of the gospel which move these people to act against any struggle for justice in this country. We believe that it is the class interest of these people, their position of dominance in our society, their being beneficiaries of this racist apartheid system, which moves them, rather than the gospel.

We are aware that there are some blacks who, having been carried by this lie preached by these groups, believe that being Christian means worrying about heavenly things alone rather than earthly things.

The only time they worry about earthly things is when they are called to defend the status quo. It is when they are called to oppose the people's struggle for justice in this country. When it comes to supporting investments they are the ones who get paraded on international platforms, sponsored by blood money, whilst they know that others are prohibited by law to challenge them.

This tendency of conservatism of evangelicals is a serious concern for us. It is a tendency which ends up on the side of the devil rather than on the side of our Lord Jesus Christ. It is an indictment against the evangelical tradition and makes us ashamed of it. It also makes it difficult to preach the evangelical faith in the townships of South Africa because this faith, this gospel of salvation, is now associated with what are called 'reactionary' forces in the townships. It is our prayer that all evangelicals should fight against this destructive conservatism of evangelicals with a godly jealousy, for the sake of the gospel of the Lord Jesus.

6. Evangelicalism and Ecumenism

Before we deal with this theme we need to explain what we mean by this word ecumenical or ecumenism. The word 'ecumenism' comes from the Greek *oikoumene,* which means the whole inhabited world. Its usage today refers to the world-wide rapprochement among the churches. It describes the process of becoming aware of each other and the attempts to draw closer together. This word has since been used to describe those churches which were willing to participate in this process against those who were not.

Although evangelicals participated in laying a foundation for the twentieth century ecumenical movement, which is now expressed in the form of local Councils of Churches, the World Council of Churches and various other federations and associations of churches, most evangelical groups pulled out of the ecumenical movement in protest against what they saw as humanism and what they called the 'social gospel' within the ecumenical movement. To most evangelicals, evangelism is a priority over and above social needs of the world. To them the greatest need of humanity is his/her spiritual need, the need to be born again, to be filled with the Holy Spirit and to live as Christ did. Social responsibility is of secondary importance, as a by the way, whilst preaching the gospel, or as a means to reach the world.

This separation between evangelicals and the so-called ecumenicals is most evident in the South African church scene today almost on the same basis.

We believe that salvation and social change cannot be separated from one another. We believe that God loved the world as a whole when he gave his only begotten son, Jesus Christ. We believe that the saving act of God is directed not only at individuals but at the whole creation. If the sin of Adam is responsible for corruption and evil in the world, if this original sin is responsible for the chaos in the world, for the wars and rumours of wars, for injustices and oppressive systems, for economic exploitation, then the saving act of Jesus must deal with this whole spectrum of the consequences of the original sin. It must deal with both the spiritual and the political socio-economic realities of the world in which we live.

There is no way therefore in which evangelism can be restricted to the so-called spiritual needs of the society. The opposite also applies that there is no way in which evangelism can be reduced to social involvement without the need for a radical change of heart of humanity. The call to be 'born again' still holds. The call to new life, new creation, where the old has passed away, is still valid. The call to righteousness, to Christian morality that is based on just actions and conduct, still stands. The fact is that the gospel does call for high Christian morality and ethics which can never be mistaken.

We believe that socal change does not guarantee the salvation of individuals as much as we do not believe that the salvation of individuals guarantees social change.

We believe that these two dimensions of the ministry of the church should always be put in balance. In fact they should be collapsed into one. The language of the 'two shall be one' should not cause difficulties for us who believe in the mystery of the trinity (the one triune God), the mystery of marriage (where the two become one) and in the mystery of salvation (where Jesus becomes one with us). This is a general concern of God to save the whole creation in its totality.

But the most startling part of this question of evangelicalism and ecumenism is that even evangelicals find it difficult to relate to one another. One finds various forms of ecumenical structures between the so-called ecumenical churches. Structures like the Council of Churches with the Catholics as observers in these structures: structures like federations of churches, theological institutions (federal seminaries) and various other structures at various other levels of the life of the church. Within the so-called evangelicals there is very little ecumenical activity or fellowship between them. For instance there is no particular relationship between the Baptists and the Apostolic Faith Mission or between these and the Assemblies of God and other groups. Even youth groups which started as interdenominational tend to be sectarian (or parochial) at the end.

The question is why evangelicals find it difficult to have fellowship with one another. Some of the reasons advanced were: dogmatism, purism (i.e. holier than thou attitude), the belief that one has the whole truth against everyone else, the problem of individualism (individual faith) as against community faith, their ecclesiology (i.e. their view of the church and understanding biblically), a ghetto theology, fear of being influenced and misled, etc.

There may be various other reasons for the tendency of 'antiecumenism' or being against ecumenical relationships amongst evangelicals. We feel that it is important to investigate (research) this area. We feel that this spirit amongst us which makes fellowship and joint efforts together difficult is responsible for our failure to minister effectively to a society at war. We need to broaden our base through ecumenical co-operation to meet both spiritual and social needs of all the people of South Africa.

7. Evangelistic Groups and Mission Theology

One unique thing about evangelicals is that they believe in undertaking mass evangelistic campaigns, in tents, stadiums, etc. and revival services in the churches. They are committed to the 'Great Commission' as they call it, to 'go into all the world and preach the gospel to the whole creation' (Mark 16:15). They are committed to making disciples of all nations, teaching them to observe all that the Lord commanded them to observe (Matt. 28:18–20). They take the promise of the Lord seriously that when the Holy Spirit has come upon them they shall be His witnesses in Jerusalem and in all Judea and Samaria and to the end of the earth (Acts 1:8).

Because of this commitment they have formed evangelistic crusades, associations and groups to undertake this mission. The various evangelical and Pentecostal Churches and youth groups also have their own evangelistic groups for this purpose.

Although we are also committed to mission and evangelism of the world (howbeit in a broader sense) we are concerned about the interests of some of these groups and their motivation to undertake this mission. Whilst we applaud and welcome their outreach drives, and their evangelistic ministry, praising God for the preaching of the gospel, we have, nevertheless some concerns to express about some of them.

Motives for Preaching the Gospel

Although we are committed to preaching the gospel to extend the Kingdom of God we are concerned about the motives of many groups for undertaking evangelistic missions. Many evangelical churches and evangelistic groups, especially those organized by whites (here or in the U.S.A.) preach the gospel to *blacks* to make them *submissive* to the oppressive apartheid system of South Africa. Some preach to blacks to make sure *they do not steal from their bosses* whilst they are responsible for underpaying them. In some cases bosses preach the gospel or invite evangelists to preach the gospel to their black workers (employees) to make sure that *they do not demand their rights as workers* particularly as regards just pay. They preach to make workers feel that it is sin to complain about unequal pay for equal work between whites and blacks.

But what is worse today is that most of these groups undertake these campaigns with the aim of *combatting* what they call '*communism*' or '*terrorism*'. They are convinced that the western capitalist culture is a Christian culture and that all forms of socialism which they call communist are atheistic and therefore anti-Christian. Most American-based crusades and American-influenced crusades, for instance, see their mission as that of promoting the West against the East. Winning souls to capitalism has become equal to winning souls for Christ; to them the West represents the Church and the East represents the mission field.

For us who are brutalized by white Christians in South Africa, with the western tradition of oppression and exploitation, for us who are oppressed and exploited by white Christians who are supported by the so-called Christian West, for us who have been called 'communists' because we resisted apartheid and oppression, for some of us who have been detained in solitary confinement under the so-called 'Terrorism' Act just for raising our voices against apartheid, for us this motive can only be seen to be coming from the devil. For us they must be held in suspicion, so that we may question the particular interests of these groups.

We as 'Concerned Evangelicals' have been outraged by the blatant way in which some North American evangelists come here to South Africa in the midst of our pain and suffering, even unto death, and pronounce that 'apartheid is dead' simply because they address a multi-racial gathering at a stadium or maybe for a more serious reason of the need to support South Africa because it profits the West at our expense. After declaring the State of Emergency on June 12, 1986, the South African T.V. replayed one North American Evangelist's sermon for South Africans to justify the silencing of the oppressed majority in South Africa and declaring a news black-out to be able to kill and detain without being monitored by the international community.

This sermon called on South Africans to promote and defend so-called western civilization, western freedoms and democracy. Many black South Africans were outraged by this sermon and the arrogance of a foreigner who comes to tell us that apartheid is dead when we know that it is alive and well, and that it kills.

We are also concerned, in the same way, about the sermons of other preachers which assume the same tone presenting white South Africa as almost the chosen one of God to fight against 'communism'. One could go on with many others here at home. It is for this reason that young evangelicals in Soweto have protested against some evangelistic missions in Soweto not because they are against the mission, per se, but because of the outrageous motives which hurt blacks in this country.

We are concerned that some of these groups are blatantly *capitalistic* and *materialistic*. They preach the gospel of prosperity claiming that this 'blessed' capitalism is from God by faith if one believes the Scriptures, confesses them and claims possessions (material) desired! What a false 'God of materialism'! This sounds like real idolatry of mammon!

Actually we 'Concerned Evangelicals' feel that these sort of groups benefit from apartheid! The riches of whites created by apartheid, at the expense of blacks, are 'blessed' by these groups as gifts from God received by faith. Many of those who claim these blessings of material possessions acquire such at the expense of others, particularly the black exploited worker of South Africa which exploitation is made possible by apartheid.

The Origins of these Groups are Suspect

One thing that has become clear nowadays is the fact that most, if not all of these groups, originate from outside South Africa, that is either from Britain, the continent of Europe or the U.S.A. Usually the origins of these evangelistic groups, seem to us to be suspect regarding their theological basis for mission and evangelization of the world. For instance, their prominent evangelists are often, if not always, *whites,* who claim they are called by God for Africa, in particular for South African blacks. Some questions arise in our minds, 'Are whites the only people who are nearer God, and therefore can easily hear God call them to his ministry, or detect God's call to minister to blacks in Africa?' 'Are the black people the only sinners on earth, to warrant such a flood of white missionaries and evangelists from America?'

White Domination

Often these groups are dominated by white Christians. Their committees are imbalanced, as to their racial composition. Even if they had a black majority it would be a token majority whilst the influence and decision-making authority remains with whites. Ideas, structures and policy are determined, both psychologically and practically, by white Christians. And because of this domination of whites, who have no understanding of the happenings in the black townships, their evangelistic mission has been disastrous and in some cases aborted in the townships.

Support for Apartheid

We are distressed when we notice that these groups are ready supporters of apartheid and its apartheid officials. Some Christian (born-again) soldiers get involved in South African Defence Force shootings in our townships, and give testimonies of Christ-inspired victory over 'communists' during church services. We regret their claim to the same faith as us, their prey! Some even prophesy that God is on the side of white racist South Africa, giving them a message of hope for victory against blacks in this country.

Almost all of them practise apartheid. They hold separate services, for 'different race groups' based on mythical claims of *language* and cultural difference—as though all whites speak the same language! Are there no Portuguese, Afrikaners, or French? Why do they not practise the same apartheid amongst themselves for the same reason?

But the most blatant symbol of support for apartheid South Africa and American values is that of the two flags which are hoisted at the Rhema Centre in Randburg, Johannesburg. Blacks who tried to go to the Centre have been greeted by the American and South African flags rather than the flag of the Kingdom of God.

This shows the degree of insensitivity of evangelical groups and their ignorance about the attitudes of most blacks in the townships. It seems that business people will always be ahead of us in terms of marketing skills and techniques and we will always lag behind. The fact of the matter is that the flag of America symbolizes 'enemy number one' in the minds of most blacks in the townships whilst that of South Africa is an insult to their humanity and dignity. It is for this reason that it is absolutely urgent to bring down those flags to replace them with the flag of the Kingdom of God for the sake of the gospel of the Lord in South Africa.

Our Theology of Mission and Evangelism

The tendencies we have referred to above have made the preaching of the gospel in our country more difficult for those of us who are called into this situation. These tendencies have reinforced the perceptions of some blacks that God is a God of the white oppressors and that the church is a western institution used by the western countries to keep blacks in subjugation. These tendencies in fact indirectly encourage more interest in the very communism these groups so fear and preach against.

We believe that unless evangelicals broaden and deepen their conception of mission and evangelism their ministry is doomed in this country. We need to accept that whereas we are called to preach the gospel in the world so that many can be saved to be able to enter into the Kingdom of God, to acquire eternal life, these very people who have accepted the Lord still have to live in this world. Before Jesus Christ comes we are to live our lives in this very world.

The question is whether we then become mere spectators in this sinful world or through our new perception of life, because of the gracious gift of God, we become a witness as to what real life is and show what it means to live life more abundantly. Do we have any contribution to make to this gloomy world or not? Do we have a ministry to it or not?

We believe that God loves this whole world and that God has called us to minister to this whole world. We are called to minister to both the spiritual and social needs of the world. We believe that one cannot meet the spiritual needs of people effectively if this does not touch on or have any bearing on their social needs. Evangelism therefore cannot be separated from social action and social justice. In fact evangelism and social action go hand in glove. If we bear the name of evangelicals we have to be true to our name by preaching good news to the poor, by proclaiming liberty to the captives and recovery of sight to the blind, by setting at liberty those who are oppressed, and by proclaiming the favourable year of the Lord (Luke 4:18–19).

8. Radicalism and Evangelicalism

By now it should be obvious that we have been trapped in the subtle forms of a false theological stance. Our faith is not conservative in the same way as we practise it. It is true that we, Christians, must conserve the Truth, our God-given life, and love-motivated goodness, and all other godly or Christlike virtues. But it is not true that we must then conserve evil ideologies such as apartheid and exploitative economic systems like the operation of capitalism in the South African context. We should not conserve a corrupt and sinful political order of the day simply because it gives us an opportunity to preach the 'spiritual' Gospel, especially for wrong reasons.

To try to extract some 'spiritual life' from a political or economic life, in the name of 'non-involvement' in politics is dualism. This dualism outlook on life is unscriptural. Life is a whole. A 'born-again' Christian was not exempted from carrying a 'pass' book, with its evil accompaniments! This is a political issue. Then why step aside when this miniature symbol of apartheid oppression, called the 'dompas', is attacked? Yet one accepts it without questioning. Perhaps we think of this as a blessed hypocrisy!

We need to ask God to help us to see, hear, and speak out! We need to find out the nature and essence of the Gospel of 'repentance and remission of sins', we have received. Is it conservative and dualistic? Does Christianity mean marriage with the government of the day? Is our evangelical faith radical or liberal? Does it call for uncompromising righteousness or for compromised moderation?

Repentance: A Radical Demand for Change

It is a maxim that to be an evangelical means to believe in repentance of one's sin(s) and conversion. It means to believe in salvation by faith alone in the Lord Jesus Christ.

It is also equally true that in our proclamation of the gospel, we condemn sin in all its forms: personal, collective and structural. We then also call people to repentance, with the hope of forgiveness of sin, and restoration of relationship with God and with people.

Whereas the word repentance (Greek, *metanoia*), means a change of mind, attitude or course, its emphasis seems to be the view to hope. In other words, one ought to repent of one's sin(s), with a view to entering into new life or relationship. It should however, be clear that this does not mean that the fact of sin is undermined or underplayed. Rather, sin is exposed and condemned. The aim being to see a totally changed life.

We therefore need to realize that a call to repentance is a call to a radical change. It is a call to a radical break with sin. A radically new life is expected from a penitent sinner, after repentance, confession and forgiveness. 2 Cor. 5:17, is a case in point. A person 'in Christ', is a new person. The old is past. The new has come. Is this not a radical fundamental change? What about the transformation that St. Paul of Tarsus is speaking of in Rom. 12:2? It is transformation by the renewal of the mind to make out what the will of God is in our lives.

Repentance: A Comprehensive Demand for Change

The problem with us (evangelicals) is that we became very radical and uncompromising against a well-selected set of sins while ignoring the rest for reasons that are not clear to many. We preach vociferously against adultery, fornication, drunkenness, thieves, robbers, hatred but are completely silent about the sin of discrimination and the sin of apartheid. We close our eyes to texts like 'God shows no partiality' (Acts 10:34). We do not see the sin of building walls of hostility between blacks and whites like the Jews did between them and the Gentiles (Eph. 2:11–22). We forget that the New Testament talks about the fact that there is no more Jew or Greek, slave or free, male or female for we were baptized in one Spirit into the one body of Christ and were all made to drink of one Spirit (1 Cor. 12:13; Gal. 3:28; Col. 3:11 etc). We are silent about the sin of oppression and exploitation. We dishonour the poor and honour the rich (James 2), contrary to the word of God.

It is clear, therefore, that our radicalism is selective radicalism. When one goes through the sins emphasized and those which are de-emphasised one can see a particular class bias. The obvious drunkards, thieves and robbers are members of a particular class of people that is likely to be oppressed, deprived, underpaid, etc., while the sins that are not emphasized are the sins of the rich, the oppressors, the exploiters, etc. There is therefore a definite bias in our sermons and message of salvation which is directed mainly at blacks rather than whites. Whites can remain racists who undermine and dehumanize blacks and still be regarded as 'fantastic' Christians. At the worst they would even speak and sing in tongues to the glory of God whilst they are responsible for the misery of millions of people in our country. At best we can only preach sermons which assure them against communists, meaning their victims of oppression and exploitation.

We as evangelicals need to repent of this selective radicalism and biased morality. We need to go back to the great Commission that calls us to preach the gospel to the whole world: to Gentiles and Jews alike, to Whites and Blacks alike, bearing in mind all the time that our God is not an impartial God. We must begin to preach vociferously against structural and institutionalized sins, like the sin of apartheid, etc. It is strange that we do preach against tribal attitudes (between Tswanas and the Zulus, between the Shangaans and the Sothos, etc.) but we seldom preach about the attitudes between Whites and Blacks, between white missionaries and black pastors. Is it because those who led this mission were whites and therefore geared the emphasis of our sermons in our training away from their own sins and focused them on us alone. Was this not a great cover-up for their own sins?

A Radical Gospel at Loggerheads with Apartheid

There are many areas at which the radical gospel we are preaching becomes at loggerheads with apartheid in South Africa and its unjust laws. Converts who have repented from the sin of racism cannot be allowed to live where they choose to live, to break away from the structural sin of separation of races in this country. The restrictions on movements of blacks seriously affects their evangelistic machinery to reach out to more souls. The suppressive security legislations inhibit the open preaching of the gospel lest one is prepared to be harassed and imprisoned by the apartheid security forces.

Our type of Gospel proclamation demands repentance. Our teaching is committal. Our discipleship is transformational. If in the process of preaching the Gospel and discipleship ministry we encounter legislative hindrance, what do we do? Do we obey Christ, which means disobedience to these laws? Or do we obey evil laws that hinder the preaching of the Gospel? How do we respond or react, when we are called by God Almighty to minister to all nations (as it is scriptural) while the South African regime executive laws to permit ministry to a particular race-group only? What do we do if a host of racist legislations hinder or frustrate the Gospel ministry?

The Gospel is radical. A call by God to a prophetic ministry is often, if not always, radical. Jeremiah was called by God to minister to nations of his time. God set him 'over nations and over kingdoms, to pluck up and to break down, to destroy and to overthrow, to build and to plant' (Jer. 1:10).

This constitutes a call and commission to a radical ministration. We have not done this. We have rather regrettably betrayed the faith. We have cowardly 'sold out' the mission of our Lord, we have sold out our birth right. We have mismanaged our responsibility. WE MUST REPENT AND MINISTER ACCORDING TO OUR CALLING.

We call upon all committed evangelicals in South Africa to come out boldly to be witnesses of the gospel of salvation, justice and peace in this country without fear. You have not received the spirit of slavery to fall back into fear (Rom. 8:15) as many of us have done. We have to take a stand now even if it may mean persecution by earthly systems. For if we fail now we shall have no legitimacy in the post-liberation period unless we want to join the hypocrites of this world.

9. Declaration

We the undersigned hereby humbly present this 'Evangelical Witness in South Africa' which we hope will help to create more awareness among evangelicals about the crisis we are facing and begin to wrestle with God, like Jacob, to determine what our role and ministry should be in this crisis situation, and how we live our faith in this situation.

1. Mr. Aubrey Adams   Baptist Church
2. Mr. Mandla Adonis   Swedish Alliance
3. Mr. D. Alie   Apostolic Faith Mission
4. Rev. Banda   Hervormde Kerk
5. Mr. Raymond Bila   Students Christian Fellowship

6.	Rev. P. Botas	Apostolic Faith Mission
7.	Mr. Petros Caku	Interdenominational Youth Christian Club
8.	Mr. Mike Chabelo	Baptist Church
9.	Rev. Frank Chikane	Apostolic Faith Mission
10.	Mr. Graham Cyster	Baptist Church
11.	Rev. Dariets	Baptist Church
12.	Mr. Mike Deka	Baptist Church
13.	Mr. Charles Dickson	Baptist Church
14.	Rev. T. Dingiswayo	Baptist Church
15.	Mr. Don B. Diphoko	Interdenominational Youth Christian Club
16.	Rev. E. Dlangamendla	Swedish Holiness Church
17.	Rev. L. Duw	Apostolic Faith Mission
18.	Mr. E. Gradwel	Apostolic Faith Mission
19.	Mr. Delby Hams	Hospital Christian Fellowship
20.	Dr. M. Hendricks	Apostolic Faith Mission
21.	Mr. T. Herbet	Apostolic Faith Mission
22.	Mr. Justice Hlatswayo	Ebenezer Evangelical Church
23.	Mr. D. Jafta	Apostolic Faith Mission
24.	Rev. Jim Johnston	Congregational Church
25.	Mr. F. Joseph	Apostolic Faith Mission
26.	Rev. Frans Kekana	International Assemblies of God
27.	Rev. K. Kgangalo	International Assemblies of God
28.	Mrs. Eva Kgoele	International Assemblies of God
29.	Rev. Louis Khomphelo	International Assemblies of God
30.	Mr. Elliot Khosana	Mamelodi Youth Christian Action
31.	Rev. Victor Khumalo	African Evangelical Church
32.	Mr. Moss Koka	Apostolic Faith Mission
33.	Ms. S. Kubatsi	
34.	Rev. John Lamula	Baptist Church
35.	Rev. I. L. Lapoorta	Apostolic Faith Mission
36.	Rev. P. Lapoorta	Apostolic Faith Mission
37.	Mr. Gordon Lebelo	International Assemblies of God
38.	Mr. Ephrem Leboa	International Youth Christian Club
39.	Dr. Henry Leberle	University of South Africa
40.	Mr. Ramotse Lehupela	International Christian Youth Club
41.	Ms. R. M. Lekgema	Assemblies of God
42.	Mr. Moses Lempe	New Life Christian Fellowship
43.	Rev. Liphoko	Apostolic Faith Mission
44.	Mr. Andre Louw	Calvinist Church
45.	Rev. Fakazi Mabaso	International Assemblies of God
46.	Rev. Jacob Mabaso	Church of England
47.	Mr. Simon Mabelane	Assemblies of God
48.	Mr. Tumelo Mabiletsa	African Evangelical Church
49.	Mr. Sipho Mabusela	Baptist Church
50.	Mr. Bheki Madolo	Apostolic Faith Mission
51.	Mr. Ephrem Mafatshe	The Outreach Christian Youth Club
52.	Mr. Pat Mahlambi	International Assemblies of God
53.	Rev. Elijah Mahlangu	Baptist Church
54.	Rev. Gideon Makhanya	Baptist Church

55.	Mr. Blyeth Makhoana	Youth Alive Ministries
56.	Mr. John Maloma	Apostolic Faith Mission
57.	Rev. Maluleke	Apostolic Faith Mission
58.	Mr. Jacob Maluleke	Seventh Day Adventists
59.	Rev. A. Malungwane	International Assemblies of God
60.	Rev. S. Mandean	Apostolic Faith Mission
61.	Mr. Enoch Maseko	International Assemblies of God
62.	Mr. Lesego Masoko	Apostolic Faith Mission
63.	Rev. George Matoboge	Baptist Church
64.	Rev. Andrew Matlhabe	International Assemblies of God
65.	Mr. Abie Matlou	Youth Alive Ministries
66.	Mr. Nkosana Mavuso	Apostolic Faith Mission
67.	Mr. Mzwakhe Mbuli	Apostolic Faith Mission
68.	Mrs. Dorah Mdluli	Tswelelopele Youth Fellowship
69.	Mr. Giyani T. Mdluli	Tswelelopele Youth Fellowship
70.	Dr. Z. Mlisana	Congregational Church
71.	Rev. Patrick Mncube	The Body of Christ
72.	Ms. N. Moabi	Students Christian Fellowship
73.	Mr. Phala Modise	Disciples Youth Fellowship
74.	Mr. Jerry Mofokeng	Youth Alive Ministries
75.	Mr. P. Mofomme	Apostolic Faith Mission
76.	Mrs. Anna Mogase	Baptist Church
77.	Mr. Dan Mogase	Baptist Church
78.	Rev. A. Mohlomonyane	Baptist Church
79.	Rev. Hiazial Mokoka	Sceptre for Justice and Peace
80.	Rev. Caesar Molebatsi	Ebenezer Evangelical Church
81.	Mr. Gilbert Molife	International Assemblies of God
82.	Mr. Bonny Molokoane	Young Adults Fellowship
83.	Mr. Vincent Monene	Mamelodi Youth for Christian Action
84.	Rev. Michael Moore	Methodist Church
85.	Rev. D. Moos	Apostolic Faith Mission
86.	Mr. C. Morah	Apostolic Faith Mission
87.	Rev. Morake	International Assemblies of God
88.	Mr. Jacob Mosime	Youth Alive Ministries
89.	Rev. K. H. Motsepe	International Assemblies of God
90.	Rev. Jerry Motsweni	
91.	Mr. Mike Moyokolo	
92.	Rev. Vincent Mpinda	Baptist Church
93.	Mr. L. Nevhutelu	Lutheran Church
94.	Rev. Zwo Nevhutalu	Lutheran Church
95.	Mr. Sydney Ngwenya	African Evangelical Church
96.	Rev. Lucas Ngwetjana	Full Gospel Church of God
97.	Mr. Sipho Nhlapo	The Outreach Christian Club
98.	Mrs. G. Nicholson	Baptist Church
99.	Rev. Nat Nkosi	Baptist Church
100.	Mr. George Nkuna	Full Gospel Church of God
101.	Ms. Nomthandazo	Student Christian Movement
102.	Rev. Errol Norse	Baptist Church
103.	Mr. Kabelo M. Ntlha	New Life Christian Fellowship

104.	Mrs. Khumo Ntlha	New Life Christian Fellowship
105.	Mr. Mosi Ntlha	New Life Christian Fellowship
106.	Rev. Sydney Ntuli	International Assemblies of God
107.	Mrs. M. Nzima	International Assemblies of God
108.	Mrs. Lettie Nzima	Apostolic Faith Mission
109.	Mr. John Orlkwood	Methodist Church
110.	Mr. B. Peterson	Apostolic Faith Mission
111.	Prof. Philprot	Congregational Church
112.	Mr. M. Radebe	Mahon Mission
113.	Mr. Oupa Radebe	Apostolic Faith Mission
114.	Mr Mohshe Rajuile	EBSCMA
115.	Rev. H. Ramaila	Evangelical Lutheran Church
116.	Mr. Wilfred Ramatlo	Apostolic Faith Mission
117.	Mr. A. Ramasiyane	Ebenezer Evangelical Church
118.	Rev. Ratshivhombhela	Scripture Union
119.	Rev. I. Reid	Apostolic Faith Mission
120.	Mr. Mike Sejaki	New Life Christian Fellowship
121.	Rev. Lucas Sejeng	International Assemblies of God
122.	Mr. V. Seleoane	Full Gospel Church of God
123.	Mr. Mike Sephisi	Mamelodi Youth Christian Action
124.	Mr. Bingo M. Shoro	Youth Alliance
125.	Mr. Bheki Skhosana	Youth Alive Ministries
126.	Rev. T. Thandekiso	Apostolic Faith Mission
127.	Mr. Sydney Thipe	Baptist Church
128.	Rev. J. Tselapedi	Evangelical Church
129.	Rev. Ronnie Vulture	International Assemblies of God
130.	Dr. David Whitelaw	Nazarene
131.	Rev. F. Wrench	Apostolic Faith Mission
132.	Rev. Zungu	Christian Alliance